Lion
Christmas
Favourites

Stories and Prayers
for the festive season

J.

Christmas Stars

The stars that shine at Christmas
Shine on throughout the year;
Jesus, born so long ago,
Still gathers with us here.
We listen to his stories,
We learn to say his prayer,
We follow in his footsteps
And learn to love and share.

Lois Rock

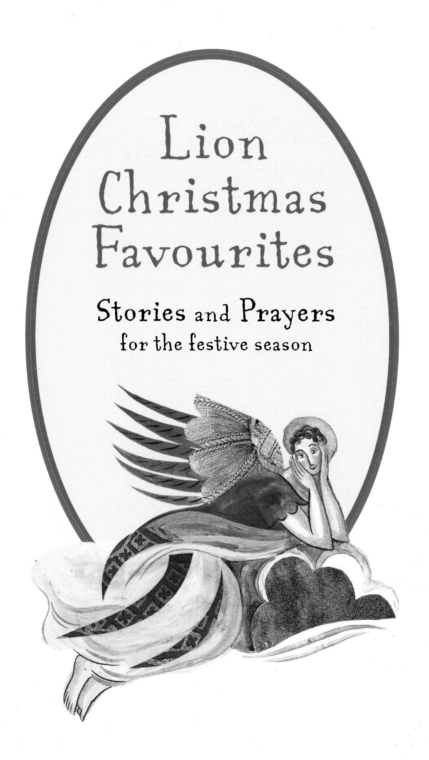

Lion Christmas Favourites

Stories and Prayers
for the festive season

LION
Children's Books

Contents

Christmas Is Coming

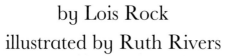

by Lois Rock

illustrated by Ruth Rivers

Dear God,

Be the flame to light my way through the dark times,

when I sit and wait for Jesus to come near.

Dear God,

Be the flame to warm my soul through the cold times,

when I sit and wait for Jesus to come near.

Dear God,

Be the flame to cheer my heart through the sad times,

when I sit and wait for Jesus to come near.

Dear God,

Be the flame to spark and sing through the silent times,

when I sit and wait for Jesus to come near.

Dear God,

May Jesus be with me this day and every day:

my light and my salvation.

I count the days to Christmas
and I watch the evening sky.
I want to see the angels
as to Bethlehem they fly.
I'm watching for the wise men
and the royal shining star.
Please may I travel with them?
Is the stable very far?
I count the days to Christmas
as we shop and bake and clean.
The lights and tinsel sparkle,
and yet deep inside I dream
that as we tell the story
of Lord Jesus and his birth,
the things of every day will fade
as heaven comes to earth.

The Story of the Nativity

retold from the Bible
illustrated by Debbie Lush

Long ago and far away, people were dreaming that one day an age of gold would dawn.

For sometimes it seemed that their lives were more bleak and dreary than any winter. Enemies had defeated their nation, and their overlords seemed cruel and unfair.

If only they could return to the times of the great King David of old, who had led their people to victory and prosperity… If only the God who had made heaven and earth would remember them, and send them a king even greater than David, who would rule with justice and righteousness, who would put an end to war, whose kingdom would never end.

Then the whole world would see that God wanted people to live freely and fairly, with kindness, compassion, justice and generosity.

The whole world would know an age of gold.

The birth of Jesus

The angel Gabriel was sent by God to a town in Galilee called Nazareth, to a young woman named Mary. She was not yet married, but she was engaged to a man named Joseph. His family could trace their ancestors back a thousand years, to a great king of their nation: King David.

'Peace be with you,' said the angel to Mary. 'The Lord is with you and has greatly blessed you.'

Mary was much perplexed. What did these words mean?

'Do not be afraid, Mary,' said the angel. 'God has chosen you to bear a son. You will name him Jesus. He will be great; he will be called the Son of the Most High, and God will make him a king like his ancestor David. His kingdom will never end.'

'How can this be?' asked Mary. 'I am a virgin – not yet married.'

'The power of God will make all this happen,' replied the angel. 'For this reason, the child to be born will be holy; he will be called the Son of God.'

Then Mary said, 'I am the Lord's servant. May it happen to me as you have said.'

The angel departed.

Mary told Joseph her news about the angel's visit and the baby she was now expecting. Joseph was dismayed and perplexed. What should he do? The baby was not his; perhaps he ought not to marry Mary.

Then, in a dream, he too was visited by an angel. 'Joseph,' said the angel, 'do not be afraid to take Mary as your wife. The child she will bear is God's holy child. You must name him Jesus, for he will rescue people and show them the right way to live.'

So Joseph took care of Mary. When the Roman emperor Augustus ordered a census of all the people who lived in his empire, Joseph took Mary with him to enter their names on the official list.

Everyone had to travel to their home town. As Joseph was descended from the nation's great King David, who had been born in Bethlehem, it was there that they made their way.

When they arrived, they found the town was crowded with people who had come to take part in the census. The inn was full. Mary and Joseph had to shelter in a stable, among the animals. There, Mary's baby son was born. She wrapped him in swaddling bands and laid him in a manger.

The shepherds on the hillsides

On the hillsides that sloped down from Bethlehem, some shepherds were spending the night outside, watching over their flocks. Suddenly, one of God's angels appeared before them, shining with all the glory of heaven.

The men cowered in fear but then the angel spoke to them:

'Do not be afraid. I come with good news: news of something that will bring joy to everyone in the world. This very day in David's town has been born a saviour, the one promised by God to lead people to freedom… the one who is to be called the Christ.

'Here is a sign for you, so you will know that what I say is true. You will find the baby wrapped in swaddling clothes and lying in a manger.'

Suddenly a great number of heaven's angels appeared, singing a song of praise: 'Glory to God in highest heaven, peace on earth and goodwill to all people.'

When the angels went back to heaven, the shepherds looked at one another with astonishment. 'Let us go to Bethlehem,' they said, 'and see for ourselves.'

So they went, and found Joseph and Mary, and the baby lying in the manger.

The shepherds told their strange story, and all who heard it were amazed. Mary thought long and deeply about every word they had said.

The shepherds went back to their flocks, singing praises to God.

The travellers from distant lands

Jesus was born in Bethlehem at the time when a man named Herod ruled as king of the Jewish people. Soon afterwards, some men who studied the stars came from lands in the east to the capital city of Jerusalem, where Herod had his palace.

The travellers were on a quest. 'Where is the baby born to be the king of the Jews?' they asked. 'We saw his star rise in the eastern skies, and we have come to worship him.'

When Herod heard this, he was disturbed and angry. He called together the learned people of his nation and spoke to them: 'Our ancient scriptures speak of a king whom God will send. Where will this king be born?'

'In Bethlehem,' they replied. 'A prophet of long ago names the very place.'

Then Herod called the travellers to a secret meeting. He wanted to know when the star had appeared. In return, he told the men to go to Bethlehem. 'Go and search for the child,' he said, 'and when you have found him, let me know, so that I too can go and worship him.'

The travellers went on their way. The star reappeared in the sky, and led them further on, until it stopped over a house in Bethlehem. There, they found the child with his mother Mary. They gave the child rich gifts: gold and frankincense and myrrh.

Afterwards, God spoke to them in a dream. 'Go back to your country by a different road,' came the warning. 'Do not go back to Herod.'

After they had left, an angel of God spoke to Joseph in a dream. 'Herod will be looking for the child,' warned the angel, 'and he wants to get rid of him. Get up now, even though it is night! Take Mary and Jesus to faraway Egypt until I tell you that it is safe to return.'

The holy family went on their way at once. Jesus was safe. He would grow to be a man, and through his life and death, he would make all of God's good promises come true.

Mary Had a Baby

A traditional West Indian carol

arranged by Philip and Victoria Tebbs
illustrated by Debbie Lush

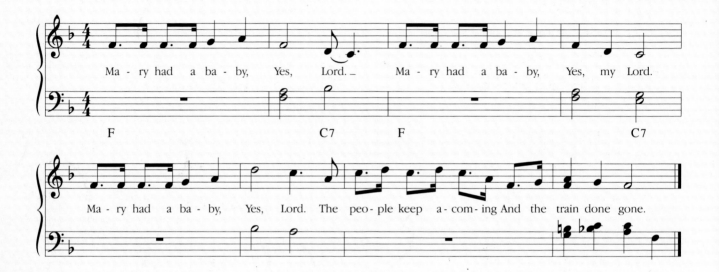

Mary had a baby,
Yes, Lord.
Mary had a baby,
Yes, my Lord.
Mary had a baby,
Yes, Lord.
The people keep a-coming
And the train done gone.*

What did she name him?
Yes, Lord.
What did she name him?
Yes, my Lord.
What did she name him?
Yes, Lord.
The people keep a-coming
And the train done gone.

* Some people sing 'Down in Bethlehem' to replace 'And the train done gone'.

Mary named him Jesus,
Yes, Lord.
Mary named him Jesus,
Yes, my Lord.
Mary named him Jesus,
Yes, Lord.
The people keep a-coming
And the train done gone.

Where was he born?
Yes, Lord.
Where was he born?
Yes, my Lord.
Where was he born?
Yes, Lord.
The people keep a-coming
And the train done gone.

Born in a stable,
Yes, Lord.
Born in a stable,
Yes, my Lord.
Born in a stable,
Yes, Lord.
The people keep a-coming
And the train done gone.

Where did Mary lay him?
Yes, Lord.
Where did Mary lay him?
Yes, my Lord.
Where did Mary lay him?
Yes, Lord.
The people keep a-coming
And the train done gone.

Laid him in a manger,
Yes, Lord.
Laid him in a manger,
Yes, my Lord.
Laid him in a manger,
Yes, Lord.
The people keep a-coming
And the train done gone.

Baby Jesus

The Christmas story retold by Lois Rock
illustrated by Alex Ayliffe

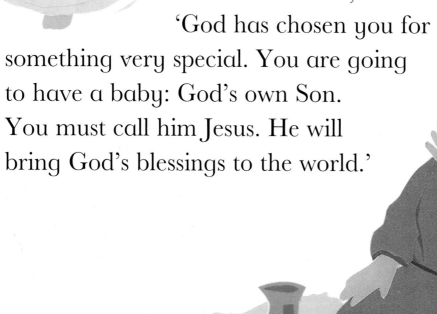

In the little town of Nazareth lived a young woman named Mary. She was looking forward to getting married.

One day, an angel came to visit her. 'Don't be afraid,' said the angel. 'God has chosen you for something very special. You are going to have a baby: God's own Son. You must call him Jesus. He will bring God's blessings to the world.'

Mary was very surprised but she agreed. 'I will do as God wants,' she said.

Mary was looking forward to marrying Joseph. But when Joseph heard Mary's news, he was worried.

Then an angel spoke to him in a dream. 'Take care of Mary,' said the angel. 'Her baby is God's own Son. He will bring God's blessings to all the world.'

Joseph was very puzzled, but he said he would take care of Mary.

And together they went to take part in a great counting of people that was being done. They went to Bethlehem.

The town was very busy. The only place to stay was in a room full of animals.

There, Mary's baby was born. Mary wrapped him in swaddling clothes. She laid him to sleep in a manger.

Out in the fields nearby, shepherds were watching their sheep. An angel appeared.

'Do not be afraid,' said the angel. 'Tonight, in Bethlehem, a baby has been born: God's special king, who will bring God's blessings to the world.'

Then all the angels sang together for joy.

The shepherds went to Bethlehem. They found Mary and the baby, just as the angel had said.

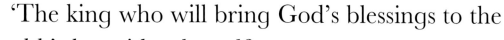

Far away, wise men saw a special star in the night sky.
'It is a sign that a new king has been born,' they said. 'We must go and find him.'

The star led them to the place where Jesus was.

They brought him gifts: gold, frankincense and myrrh.

Mary smiled. The gifts for Jesus were gifts for a king.

'The king who will bring God's blessings to the world,' she said to herself.

Little Angels

by Christina Goodings

illustrated by Alex Ayliffe

The little angels think it grand
To sit up through the night,
Watching over children
Until the morning bright.

They make themselves all neat and clean
And feel so very proud
To bring their little teddies
And snuggle on a cloud.

They bring with them a box of dreams –
Good dreams of joy and love
That float like silver stardust
To earth from heaven above.

Teddy Bear, Piglet, Kitten and Me

A Christmas poem by Catherine Maccabe
illustrated by Clive Scruton

We went to the beach, where the waves were so wild,

Much larger, dear God, than one little child:

I know we are small, but please, can you see,

Teddy bear, piglet, kitten and me?

We went to the woods, where the trees grow so high,

I can tell, if I look, that they reach to the sky:

I know we are small, but please, can you see,

Teddy bear, piglet, kitten and me?

We went to the park, where it started to rain,
There was thunder and lightning and thunder again:
I know we are small, but please, can you see,
Teddy bear, piglet, kitten and me?

We went to the zoo, where the elephants stay,
They're bigger than houses, and too big to play:
I know we are small, but please, can you see,
Teddy bear, piglet, kitten and me?

We went to the town, full of bustle and noise,
I nearly got lost in the shop that sells toys:
I know we are small, but please, can you see,
Teddy bear, piglet, kitten and me?

We went to the church, we walked through the snow,
Inside it was warm in the candlelit glow:
I know we are small, but I think you can see,
Teddy bear, piglet, kitten and me?

24

We've come to the stable, we followed the star,
Baby Jesus lies smiling, we know who you are –
God's son, oh, so small, so of course you can see,
Teddy bear, piglet, kitten and me.

Let Us Travel to christmas

Four Christmas poems
illustrated by John Wallace

Let us travel to Christmas
By the light of a star.
Let us go to the hillside
Right where the shepherds are.
Let us see shining angels
Singing from heaven above.
Let us see Mary cradling
God's holy child with love.

Lois Rock

Ox and ass at Bethlehem
On a night ye know of them;
We were only creatures small
Hid by shadows on the wall.

We were swallow, moth and mouse;
The Child was born in our house,
And the bright eyes of us three
Peeped at His Nativity.

Bruce Blunt

26

An azure sky,
All star bestrewn.
A lowly crib,
A hushèd room.
An open door,
A hill afar,
Where little lambs
And shepherds are.
To such a world,
On such a night,
Came Jesus –
Little Lord of Light.

Mary I. Osborn

Think of a gift for a baby boy:
A cuddly quilt and a special toy.

Think of a gift for a baby king:
All that the rich and the wise can bring.

Think of a gift for the baby you love:
All the blessings of God above.

Lois Rock

The Fourth Wise Man

A Christmas legend

retold by Lois Rock
illustrated by Christina Balit

Across the desert the wise men were riding... riding their camels through the dark of the night.

'See the star is leading us!' cried the first.

'Leading us to a king,' agreed the second.

'The king of heaven and earth,' added the third.

There was a fourth man with them. 'I wish I was as wise as my companions,' he said to himself. 'Then I would have known more about the reason for our journey before we set off.'

'The gift I bring is hidden in my saddlebag,' whispered the first.

'The gift I bring is strapped to my belt,' answered the second.

'The gift I bring is sewn among the folds of my tunic,' added the third.

The fourth man looked sad. 'I have not yet found a
gift worthy of the king,' he sighed. 'I am still looking.'

'My gift is gold, for a king who is powerful,'
proclaimed the first.

'My gift is frankincense, for a king whose prayers
will rise to God in heaven,' announced the second.

'My gift is myrrh, for a king who will be famous in
life and yet more famous in death,' declared the third.

The fourth man lowered his eyes. 'I don't even know what gift I would choose,' he sighed.

So the four men travelled on through the night and continued their journey for many days and many nights.

At last, the star that led them hung still in the night sky. Below it was a humble dwelling.

'This is an unusual place to find a king,' noted the first man.

'But the star clearly shows that it is the right place,' replied the second.

'So let us go in and present our gifts,' said the third.

The fourth man waited outside. 'I may as well fetch water for the camels,' he said to himself. 'I have not found a gift for the one who is within.'

He went to the well and drew a bucketful of water. It was heavy, and he set it down on the ground for a moment.

Then he saw something wonderful. He bent closer.

'The star,' he said. 'The star that is in the sky is also in my old and battered bucket.'

He gazed in delight for a moment. And then he laughed aloud.

'This is what I shall take the king,' he said, 'a reflection of the light from the heavens.'

And by a miracle, the star kept on shining in the bucket of water to make the child-king smile.

The Gifts of Christmas

Two Christmas poems by Lois Rock
illustrated by Sarah Young

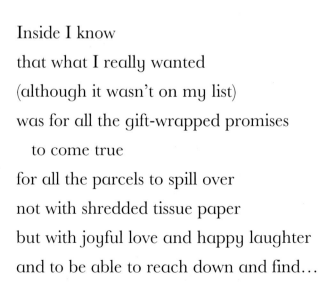

I really love Christmas Eve
when we put the presents under the tree:
a gleeful heap of promises
in red and green
gold and silver
tags and ribbons
and loads and loads of love.

And then, on Christmas Day,
there are splendid things to see:
gadgets and gizmos
toys and socks
nuts and chocolates
and foaming bath perfumes in
   exotic bottles.
But somehow the magic has gone.

Inside I know
that what I really wanted
(although it wasn't on my list)
was for all the gift-wrapped promises
   to come true
for all the parcels to spill over
not with shredded tissue paper
but with joyful love and happy laughter
and to be able to reach down and find…

Christmas!

'For Christmas would you like some gold?'
I'd rather just have money.
'And what about some frankincense?'
Come on, you're being funny.

And what is more, I don't want… 'No!
I've gone and bought the myrrh!'
You could have asked me for a list
of things that I'd prefer.

'You're not exactly Jesus then?'
Oh, no. I'm plain old me.
And I want fairly normal gifts
left underneath the tree:

I'll have this season's latest fad,
to be like all my friends
And chocolate that will last me, oh,
at least till this year ends.

'But Christmas gifts should be much more –
they should have lasting worth.'
May I suggest good will to all
and maybe peace on earth.

Baboushka

A traditional Russian folktale

retold by Arthur Scholey
illustrated by Ray and Corrine Burrows

All the villagers were out, bubbling with excitement.

'Did you see it again last night?'

'Of course we did.'

'Much bigger.'

'It was moving, coming towards us. Tonight it will be high above us.'

That night, excitement, like a wind, scurried through the lanes and alleys.

'There's been a message.'

'An army is on the way.'

'Not an army – a procession.'

'Horses and camels and treasure.'

Now everyone was itching for news. No one could work. No one could stay indoors.

No one that is, but Baboushka. Baboushka had work to do – she always had. She swept, polished scoured and shined. Her house was the best kept, best polished, best washed and painted. Her garden was beautiful, her cooking superb.

'All this fuss for a star!' she muttered. 'I haven't time even to look. I'm so behind, I must work all night!'

So she missed the star at its most dazzling, high overhead. She missed the line of twinkling lights coming towards the village at dawn. She missed the sound of pipes and drums, the tinkling of bells getting louder. She missed the voices and whispers and

then the sudden quiet of the villagers, and the footsteps coming up the path to her door. But the knocking! She couldn't miss that.

'Now what?' she demanded, opening the door.

Baboushka gaped in astonishment. There were three kings at her door! And a servant.

'My masters seek a place to rest,' he said. 'Yours is the best house in the village.'

'You… want to stay here?'

'It would only be till night falls and the star appears again.'

Baboushka gulped. 'Come in, then,' she said.

How the kings' eyes sparkled at the sight of the home-baked bread, the meat pies, the cakes, jams and pickles.

As she dashed about, serving them, Baboushka asked question after question.

'Have you come a long way?'

'Very far,' sighed Caspar.

'And where are you going?'

'We're following the star,' said Melchior.

'But where?'

They didn't know, they told her. But they believed that it would lead them, in the end, to a new-born king, a king such as the world had never seen before, a king of Earth and Heaven.

'Why don't you come with us?' said

Balthasar. 'Bring him a gift as we do. See, I bring gold, and my colleagues bring spices and ointments.'

'Oh,' said Baboushka. 'I am not sure that he would welcome me. And as for a gift…'

'This excellent pickle's fit for any king!' cried Balthasar.

Baboushka laughed. 'Pickle? For a baby? A baby needs toys.' She paused. 'I have a cupboard full of toys,' she said sadly. 'My baby son, my little king, died while very small.'

Balthasar stopped her as she bustled once more to the kitchen.

'This new king could be your king,

too. Come with us when the star appears tonight,' he said.

'I'll… I'll think about it,' sighed Baboushka.

As the kings slept, Baboushka cleaned and tidied as quietly as she could. What a lot of extra work there was! And this new king. What a funny idea – to go off with the kings to find him. Yet, could she possibly do it? Leave home and go looking for him just like that?

Baboushka shook herself. No time for dreaming! All this washing-up, and putting away of dishes, and extra cooking. Anyway, how long would she be away? What would she wear? And what about gifts?

She sighed. 'There is so much to do. The house will have to be cleaned when they've gone. I couldn't just leave it.'

Suddenly it was night-time again. There was the star!

'Are you ready, Baboushka?'

'I'll… I'll come tomorrow,' Baboushka called. 'I'll catch up. I must tidy here, find a gift, get ready…'

The kings waved sadly. The star shone ahead. Baboushka ran back into the house, eager to get on with her work.

Sweeping, dusting, beating all the cushions and carpets, cleaning out the kitchen, cooking – away went the night.

At last she went to the small cupboard, opened the door and gazed sadly once again at all those toys. But, goodness me, how dusty they were! One thing was certain. They weren't fit for a baby king. They would all need to be cleaned. Better get started at once.

On, on, she worked. One by one the toys glowed, glistened and gleamed. There! Now they would be fit for the royal baby.

Baboushka looked through the window. It was dawn! Clear on the air came the sound of the farm cockerel. She looked up. The star had gone. The kings would have found somewhere else to rest by now. She would easily catch them up.

At the moment, though, she felt so tired. Surely she could rest now – just for an hour.

Suddenly, she was wide awake. It was dark. She had slept all day! She ran out into the street. No star. She rushed back into the house, pulled on her cloak, hurriedly packed the toys in a basket and stumbled down the path the kings had taken.

On she went, hurrying through village after village. Everywhere she asked after the kings.

'Oh yes,' they told her, 'we saw them. They went that way.'

Days passed and Baboushka lost count. The villages grew bigger and became towns. But Baboushka never stopped, through night and day. Then she came to a city.

The palace! she thought. That's where the royal baby would be born.

'No royal baby here,' said the palace guard.

'Three kings? What about them?' asked Baboushka.

'Ah yes, they came. But they didn't stay long. They were soon on their journey.'

'But where to?'

'Bethlehem, that was the place. I can't imagine why. It's a very poor place. But that's where they went.'

She set off at once.

It was evening when Baboushka wearily arrived at Bethlehem. How many days had she been on the journey? She could not remember. And could this really be the place for a royal baby? It didn't look like it. It was not much bigger than her own village. She went to the inn.

'Oh yes,' said the landlord, 'the kings were here, two days ago. There was great excitement. But they didn't even stay the night.'

'And a baby?' Baboushka cried. 'Was there a baby?'

'Yes,' said the landlord, 'there was. Those kings asked to see the baby, too.'

When he saw the disappointment in Baboushka's eyes, he stopped.

'If you'd like to see where the baby was,' he said quickly, 'it was across the yard there. I couldn't offer the poor couple anything better at the time. My inn was packed full. They had to go in the stable.'

Baboushka followed him across the yard.

'Here's the stable,' he said. Then he left her.

'Baboushka?'

40

Someone was standing in the half-light of the doorway. He looked kindly at her. Perhaps he knew where the family had gone? She knew now that the baby king was the most important thing in the world to her.

'They have gone to Egypt, and safety,' he told Baboushka. 'And the kings have returned to their kingdoms another way. But one of them told me about you. I am sorry but, as you see, you are too late. Shepherds came as soon as the angels told them. The kings came as soon as they saw the star. It was Jesus the Christ-child they found, the world's Saviour.'

It is said that Baboushka is still looking for the Christ-child, for time means nothing in the search for things that are real. Year after year she goes from house to house calling, 'Is he here? Is the Christ-child here?'

Particularly at Christmas, when she sees a sleeping child and hears of good deeds, she will lift out a toy from her basket and leave it, just in case.

Then, on Baboushka goes with her journey, still searching, still calling, 'Is he here? Is the Christ-child here?'

The Legend of Saint Nicholas

retold by Lois Rock

illustrated by Helen Cann

The three sisters stood on tiptoe in the streets of Myra. Above the heads of the wedding guests, they could just catch a glimpse of the bride.

'What a lovely dress she has,' sighed the youngest sister.

'What a lovely party she is having,' sighed the middle sister.

'What a lovely home she will have with her husband,' sighed the eldest.

But then one of the wedding ushers came along. 'Make room for the guests; let the guests through,' he ordered. And the sisters had to slip back into the alleyway that led to their home. They had not been invited. They were too poor for the wealthy to count them as friends. They were so poor they knew their father could never afford the dowry that every girl needed if she was to get married.

Back in the tiny dwelling that was their home, they took off their wet shoes and stockings and huddled round the meagre fire of twigs.

'We shall have to beg for our living,' said the youngest sister.

'Or we shall starve,' said the middle sister.

The eldest sister remained silent. 'What can I do to earn some money for my family?' she worried. 'Will I ever get married?'

Their father returned. 'I walked the streets, taking work wherever I was needed, but this is all the food my wages could buy,' he said sadly. Together they ate a simple meal of bread and soup, trying not to think of the great feast that others were enjoying in the heart of town.

The fire soon burnt low, and night was falling. The sisters had no candle, so they left their shoes and stockings by the hearth and went to bed.

In a great hall in the centre of town, huge torches burnt to illuminate the wedding festivities. Many wealthy people had gathered in their fine clothes to celebrate the wedding. Now they were eating and drinking, singing and dancing. Among them walked a plainly dressed man named Nicholas. He was the bishop of the church and had himself performed the wedding ceremony for the young couple. Many of the guests knew him as a friend.

'My dear Nicholas,' called one man, 'thank you so much for visiting my mother when she was ill and I was away on business. Please accept this small gift with our grateful thanks.'

A woman made her way through the crowd to Nicholas. 'My son is so much happier at school now that he can read as well as the others,' she smiled. 'Thank you so much for helping him learn his letters. Please accept this small gift with our grateful thanks.'

The bride's father saw Nicholas from across the hall and strode over. 'It is a privilege to have you at our daughter's wedding,' he cried. 'We are so pleased you were able to perform the ceremony, and ask for God's blessing on my daughter and her new family.' Then, speaking more quietly, he added, 'Please accept this small gift with our grateful thanks.'

At midnight, while the party was still at its height, Nicholas slipped away into the dark streets. He made his way to the poorer part of town, where few candles flickered at the windows. He came at last to a house that was completely dark, where the three sisters lived with their father.

The wooden shutters were old and broken, and carefully Nicholas pulled one shutter open.

One. Two. Three.

Through the window, Nicholas threw the bags of gold he had been given; then, silently and unseen, he went away.

The following morning, the youngest sister woke first. 'There is a bag of gold in my shoe!' she exclaimed.

The middle sister tumbled from her bed and came to see. 'And look, here is gold in mine,' she cried.

The eldest sister came running and picked up her shoes. 'There is gold in my shoe too,' she whispered, and a tear of happiness slid down her cheeks.

She went out to buy bread and meat and fresh vegetables and wine. That day, as the family gathered around their small feast, their father stood up from the table and said proudly, 'I do not know who has brought us good fortune today; but if that person lives in this town, then they will see what I shall do with the gifts they have given. For I shall arrange a good marriage for each of you, my daughters: first my eldest daughter, second my middle daughter and third my youngest daughter.

'What is more,' he added, 'I shall even ask Bishop Nicholas to perform the wedding ceremony, and pray for God's blessing on each of you.'

Brother Comgall's Christmas

retold by Bob Hartman
illustrated by Susie Poole

Christmas was coming and Brother Comgall should have been happy. He should have been hanging decorations. He should have been planning games. He should have been making preparations for the Christmas feast that he shared with the boys in his monastery each year.

He should have been excited and filled with joy. But he wasn't. For a great famine had struck Ireland and there was almost nothing left to eat.

A little mouse crept up the side of Brother Comgall's chair, then hopped onto his desk. But Brother Comgall did not chase the mouse away. Instead, he smiled weakly and said, 'Hello, my friend.' And from his pocket he pulled a tiny bit of bread, and an even tinier piece of cheese.

The mouse began to chatter and squeak.

'What's that?' asked Brother Comgall. 'Oh, I see. You will not have any unless I eat some too? Yes, you are right. We have always shared our meals together. But there is so little, my friend. Hardly enough for you, let alone for me!'

The little mouse, however, would not be persuaded. He chattered and squeaked his protest until Brother Comgall finally broke off a bit for himself as well.

The 'meal' took hardly any time at all. And when they had finished, the mouse began to chatter again.

'Yes,' Brother Comgall nodded. 'I thought of that too. The Prince of Ulster has food to spare. But his storehouse is full because he has stolen that food from every family in his charge. He is an evil man, my friend, and I cannot believe that he would help us.'

But the mouse would not give up. He twitched his nose. He chattered and squeaked again. And Brother Comgall smiled.

'No,' he said at last. 'I suppose there would be no harm in asking.'

And with that, he said farewell to his little friend, bundled up in his warmest robe, and set off for the castle of the Prince of Ulster.

Outside it was bitterly cold. Ice hung from the trees. Snow was piled knee-deep. And the wind howled so loudly that Brother Comgall could hardly hear himself as he hummed a Christmas hymn.

Inside the castle, however, everything was warm. And as Brother Comgall entered and bowed, he found the prince and all his friends sitting behind a long table – piled high with meat and bread and pies.

'What do you want, monk?' barked the prince through a mouthful of food.

'Something to eat,' Brother Comgall answered. 'Not for myself, but for the boys – the sons of your own people whom we teach to read and write.'

'Why come to me?' the prince asked. 'You teach that your Christian god takes care of you. Why not beg from him?'

'Because you have food to spare,' Brother Comgall continued, 'but the boys have nothing.'

'The boys would be of more use to me if you taught them how to use a sword!' the prince growled. And then he rose to

his feet. 'What do I need with men who can read and write? Teach them how to kill, and then they will be worth feeding!'

Brother Comgall could stand this no longer.

'I will do no such thing!' he answered. 'I will teach them to read and to think – and to know the difference between goodness and greed. And perhaps, one day, this land will have a leader who knows how to care for his people!'

'Throw him out!' the prince ordered. So the guards grabbed Brother Comgall and threw him to the ground, outside the castle gates.

He was bruised when he got up, and bleeding too. And as Brother Comgall hobbled home, the pain in his head and legs grew worse and worse, until he collapsed in the snow in front of the monastery door. Fortunately, one of the other monks spotted him, carried him into the monastery and tucked him into bed.

Brother Comgall slept for the next three days, his body wet with the sweat of a hot fever. There were times when the other monks thought that he might never wake again. But on Christmas morning, as they huddled around his bed in prayer, Brother Comgall opened his eyes.

'What day is it?' he asked, weakly. 'Christmas Day,' they answered.

'Then what are you doing here?' he asked. 'You should be bringing the food from our storehouse and preparing the great Christmas feast!'

The monks looked at one another, worried. Perhaps the fall had rattled Brother Comgall's brains!

'But the storehouse is nearly empty!' one of the monks explained. 'Surely you remember the famine!'

'Of course I remember,' said Brother Comgall. 'But as I lay here, fighting the fever, I was praying.' And then he chuckled. 'It was the Prince of Ulster's idea, actually! And I believe that God has answered my prayers. So, go! And bring what you find.'

The monks went. And when they opened the storehouse doors, they could not believe what they saw. The room was full! Full of meat and bread and pies. So full that there was enough for the boys in the monastery that Christmas Day, and for all their families too. It was the best Christmas feast any of them could remember!

Late that night, the little mouse came to visit Brother Comgall. He crept onto the bed and scampered across the covers. As always, the monk had cheese and bread waiting for him.

'Where have you been?' he asked. 'I've missed you these last few days.'

The little mouse chattered and squeaked. And when he had finished his story, all Brother Comgall could do was shake his head in wonder.

'Have I got this right?' he said. 'One of your cousins was under the Prince's table? He heard what the Prince said to me? He saw what the Prince did to me? And so he called you and a thousand of your other cousins, and in the middle of the night, you took every bit of food from the Prince's storehouse and carried it here to the monastery?'

The little mouse nodded his head. He squeaked and he squealed and if Brother Comgall hadn't known better, he would have sworn that his little friend was giggling!

'Thank you,' said the monk. Then he bowed his head and thanked God too – for a miracle more amazing than he could ever have imagined.

And the monk and the mouse ate their little Christmas meal together.

Papa Panov's Special Day
Ruben Saillens's traditional tale for Christmas

adapted by Leo Tolstoy and retold by Mig Holder
illustrated by Tony Morris

A long time ago, almost too long ago to remember, there lived an old shoemaker. His home was far away, almost too far to imagine, in a small Russian village.

His name was Panov. But nobody called him Panov or Mister Panov or even shoemaker Panov; wherever he went in the village he was known as Papa Panov because everybody was so fond of him.

Papa Panov was not very rich – all he owned in the world was one small room looking out onto the village street. And in that one room he lived and slept and made shoes.

But neither was he very poor. He had all his shoemaking tools, a beautiful cast-iron stove to cook his food and warm his hands, a great wicker chair where he sat and snoozed, a good firm bed with a patchwork cover and a little oil lamp to see by when evening crept in. And there were so many people who wanted new shoes made, or old ones patched and soled and heeled, that Papa Panov always had enough money to buy bread from the baker's, coffee from the grocer's and cabbage to make soup for his dinner.

So Papa Panov was quite happy – most of the time. Most of the time, his eyes would sparkle through his little round spectacles and he would sing and whistle and shout a cheery greeting to people passing by.

But on this particular day it was different. Papa Panov stood sadly in the window of his little shop and thought of his wife who had died many years before and of his sons and daughters who had all grown up and gone away. It was Christmas Eve and everybody else was at home with their families. Papa Panov looked up and down the

52

village street and saw windows bright with candles and lamps and Christmas trees. He heard laughter and squeals of children playing games. And the faint smell of roasting meat crept through the cracks round the door and window of his little shop.

'Dearie, dearie,' said Papa Panov, pulling at his long grey moustache and shaking his head from side to side.

'Dearie, dearie,' and there was nobody to bring back the sparkle behind his little round spectacles.

Papa Panov sighed a great sigh. Then he slowly lit the oil lamp, went to a high shelf and lifted down an old brown book.

He dusted some scraps of leather off the bench, set a pot of coffee on the stove, sat down in the great wicker chair and began to read. Now Papa Panov had never been to school and could not read very well so, as he went, he ran his finger along the lines, saying the words out loud.

This was the story of Christmas. He read how a little boy, Jesus, was born, not in a good warm house but in a cowshed because there wasn't any room at the inn where his mother and father had asked to stay the night.

'Dearie, dearie,' said Papa Panov, pulling at his long moustache. 'If they had come here, they could have slept on my good bed and I would have covered the little boy with my patchwork quilt. I should like some company and a little child to play with.'

Papa Panov got up and poked the stove. It was becoming quite foggy outside so he turned up the lamp. He poured himself a mug of coffee and went back to his book.

He read how the rich men travelled across the desert to bring wonderful presents for the little boy Jesus – presents of gold and sweet-smelling spices.

'Dearie, dearie,' sighed Papa Panov, 'if Jesus came here, I shouldn't have anything to give him.' Then he smiled and his eyes sparkled behind his little round spectacles. He got up from the table and went over to the high shelf.

On it was a dusty box tied with string. He opened the box and unwrapped a pair of tiny shoes. Papa Panov held one small shoe in each hand and stood very still. They were the best shoes he had ever made.

He put them lovingly away in their box and lowered his old limbs back into the great wicker chair.

'That's what I would have given him,' he murmured.

He sighed a deep sigh and turned his attention to the book once more.

Now whether it was the warmth of the room or whether it was because it was getting late, who can say, but it wasn't long before Papa Panov's bony finger slid from the page, his little round spectacles slipped from his nose and he fell sound asleep.

Outside, the fog grew thicker. Dim figures glided past the window. But the old shoemaker slumbered on, snoring gently.

Suddenly, 'Papa, Papa Panov!' said a voice in the room. The old man jumped. His grey moustache quivered. 'Who is it?' he cried, looking about him vaguely. He could see so little without his spectacles, but there seemed to be no one there.

'Papa Panov,' said the voice again. 'You wished that you had seen me, that I had come to your little shop and that you could bring me a gift. Look out into the street from dawn to dusk tomorrow and I will come. Be sure you recognize me for I shall not say who I am.'

Then all was quiet. Papa Panov rubbed his eyes and sat up with a start. The charcoal in the stove had burned low and the lamp had gone out altogether but outside, bells were ringing everywhere. Christmas had come.

'It was him,' said the old man to himself. 'That was Jesus.' He pulled at his moustache thoughtfully. 'Perhaps it was a dream – no matter, I will watch and hope that he will visit me on Christmas Day. But how shall I know him? He was not always a little boy; he grew to be a man, a king; they said he was God himself.'

The old man shook his head, 'Dearie, dearie,' he said slowly, 'I shall have to look very carefully.'

Papa Panov did not go to bed that night. He sat in his wicker chair, facing the window, and kept watch for the very first person to pass that way. Little by little the sun's rays crept up over the hill and began to brighten the long cobbled street outside.

Nobody was coming yet.

'I'll just make a nice pot of coffee for my Christmas breakfast,' said Papa Panov to himself cheerfully. 'I'll stoke up the charcoal in the stove and brew a huge jug of steaming coffee, but I'll keep an eye on the window all the while. I hope he will come today.'

So Papa Panov waited.

At last there was someone: a figure came into view at the far end of the winding road. Papa Panov pressed his face to the frosty glass. He was very excited – perhaps this was Jesus coming to see him. Then he stepped back, disappointed. The figure was coming closer, trudging slowly up the street, stopping every now and then. Papa

Panov knew who it was – the old roadsweeper who came each week with his barrow and broom.

Papa Panov felt cross. He had better things to do than watch out for an old roadsweeper. He was waiting for God, for the King, Jesus. He turned away from the window impatiently and waited till he thought the old fellow had passed by. But when he turned back, the roadsweeper was there on the other side of the road opposite Papa Panov's shop. He had set down his barrow and was rubbing his hands together and stamping his feet. Papa Panov felt sorry. The poor roadsweeper *did* look very cold. And imagine having to work on Christmas Day!

Papa Panov tapped on the window but the old fellow did not hear. So he went and opened the door of the little shop.

'Hey!' he called from the doorway. 'Hey old chap!' The roadsweeper looked round anxiously – people were often very rude to him because of his job – but Papa Panov was smiling.

'How about a cup of coffee,' he called. 'You look frozen to the bone.' The roadsweeper left his barrow at once.

'Don't mind if I do,' he said, shuffling into the tiny shop. 'It's very kind of you, very kind.'

Papa Panov poured out a mug of coffee from the jug on the stove.

'It's the least I can do,' he said, over his shoulder. 'After all it *is* Christmas.'

The old fellow sniffed. 'Well, this is all the Christmas I'll get.' As he warmed himself at the stove, thin drifts of steam rose from his damp clothes making a sour smell in the room.

Papa Panov returned to his place at the window and gazed up and down the street.

'You expecting visitors?' asked the old roadsweeper gruffly. 'Not in the way, am I?'

Papa Panov shook his head. 'I… Well, have you heard of Jesus?' he asked.

'The Son of God?' asked the old man.

'He's coming today,' replied Papa Panov.

The old man looked at him in astonishment.

So Papa Panov told him the whole story.

'So that's why I'm watching out for him,' he finished at last.

The roadsweeper set down his mug, shook his head gloomily, and made for the door. 'Well, the best of luck,' he said, 'and, em, thanks for the coffee.' For the first time, the roadsweeper smiled. Then he hurried off into the street collecting his barrow as he went.

Papa Panov stood in the open doorway and watched the roadsweeper disappear.

He looked up and down the street. The winter sun was shining brightly and its rays even gave off a little warmth which was melting the frost on the window and the slippery ice on the cobblestones.

People were beginning to stir; a few drunks staggered home after the parties of the night before. Families in smart clothes hurried on their way to visit relatives. They nodded and smiled at Papa Panov as he stood on the threshold of his shop.

'Merry Christmas, Papa Panov,' they called. And the old shoemaker nodded and smiled back but he did not stop them… he knew them all by name. He was waiting for someone else.

He was just about to shut the door and go inside when something caught his eye. Stumbling along in the shadows close to the wall was a young woman carrying a baby. She was very thin, her face was tired and her clothes were shabby.

Papa Panov watched her. Suddenly he called out, 'Hello, why don't you come in and warm yourself?' She looked up startled and made as if to run away. But she saw the old shoemaker's eyes sparkling behind his spectacles.

'You're very kind,' she said, as he stood aside for her to enter his little shop. Papa Panov shrugged.

'No, not really,' he said, 'you just looked so cold. Have you got far to go?'

'To the next village,' she replied flatly. 'About four miles. I used to lodge down at the mill but I have no money left to pay the rent. So I must go and ask my cousin to take me in. I have no husband, you see.'

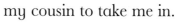

The woman went inside and stood by the stove. Papa Panov took the baby in his arms. 'Will you share some bread and soup with me?' he asked. But the woman shook her head proudly.

'Well, some milk for the child then,' he said. 'I'll heat some on the stove. Don't worry' – his eyes sparkled – 'I've had children of my own!' The child chuckled and kicked his feet.

'Dearie, dearie,' said Papa Panov, shaking his head, 'the poor mite has no shoes.'

'I've none to give him,' said the young woman bitterly.

As Papa Panov sat feeding the little

boy a thought came into his mind. He pushed it away – but it came back. The box from his high shelf! The pair of tiny shoes he had made so long ago – they might fit the baby.

So Papa Panov got them down from the shelf and tried them on the child's feet. They fitted exactly. Perfect!

'There; you can have these,' he said softly. The young woman was overjoyed. 'How can I thank you enough?' she cried.

But Papa Panov didn't hear. He was looking anxiously out of the window. Had Jesus gone by while he was feeding the child?

'Something the matter?' asked the young woman kindly.

'Have you heard of Jesus who was born at Christmas?' replied the old shoemaker.

The girl nodded.

'He's coming today,' said Papa Panov,

'he promised.' And he told her all about the dream – if it was a dream.

The young woman listened until he had finished. She looked as if she didn't believe him at all, but she patted the old shoemaker's hand kindly.

'Well, I hope your dream comes true,' she said. 'You deserve it, for being so good to me and the baby.'

And with that she went on her way.

Papa Panov closed the door behind her and, after boiling up a big dish of cabbage soup for his dinner, took up his place at the window once again.

Hours ticked by and people came and went. Papa Panov looked closely at everyone who passed. But Jesus did not come.

Then he began to be afraid. Perhaps Jesus had come and he had not recognized him. Perhaps he had passed by quickly when Papa Panov had turned away just for a second to poke the fire or boil the soup! The old shoemaker could sit still no longer. He went to the door of the little shop for one last look.

All sorts of people came by, children and old men, beggars and grannies, cheerful people and grumpy people; to some he gave a smile, to some a nod and to the beggars a coin or a hunk of bread.

But Jesus did not come.

As dusk fell and the grey December fog began creeping up again, the old shoemaker sadly lit his oil lamp and sat down wearily in the great wicker chair. He took out his book to read, but his heart was too heavy and his eyes were too tired to make out the words on the page.

'It was only a dream after all,' he said to himself sadly. 'I wanted to believe it so much; I wanted him to come.'

And two great tears welled up behind his spectacles and filled his eyes, so that he could hardly see.

At once it seemed as if there was someone in the room. Through his tears Papa Panov seemed to see a long line of people passing across the little shop.

The roadsweeper was there and the woman with her child – all the people he had seen and spoken to that day.

And as they passed they whispered, one by one, 'Didn't you see me? Didn't you see me, Papa Panov?'

'Who are you?' cried the old shoemaker, struggling out of his chair, 'Who are you? Tell me.'

And there came the same voice as the night before, though where it came from, Papa Panov could not have said.

'I was hungry and you gave me food, I was thirsty and you gave me water, I was cold and you took me in. These people you have helped today – all the time you were helping them, you were helping me!'

Then everything was quiet.

The tears dried in the old man's eyes and there was no one to be seen.

'Dearie, dearie,' said Papa Panov slowly, pulling at his long grey moustache. 'So he came after all.'

The old shoemaker shook his head from side to side thoughtfully. Then he smiled and the sparkle came back behind his little round spectacles.

Heaven on Earth

illustrated by Christopher Corr

Somehow, not only for Christmas,
But all the long year through,
The joy that you give to others,
Is the joy that comes back to you.
And the more you spend in blessing
The poor and lonely and sad,
The more of your heart's possessing
Returns to you glad.

John Greenleaf Whittier

O God,

We give thanks for the goodhearted
people who love us and do good to us
and who show their mercy and
kindness by providing us with food and
drink, house and shelter when we are in
trouble or in need.

From a 1739 prayer book

May the world turn round about,
may all things turn to right;
may the sunset thank the dawn,
the noontime bless the night.

May the rivers thank the rain,
the stormclouds bless the sea;
may the good soil thank the leaves,
the sunshine bless the tree.

May the rich thank those in need,
the children bless the old;
may the strong thank those who fail,
the timid bless the bold.

May the angels sing on earth,
may heaven hear our prayer;
may forgiveness, joy and peace
be here and everywhere.

Lois Rock

Compiled by Lois Rock
Design by Nicky Jex Design
Hardback edition copyright © 2004 Lion Hudson
Paperback edition copyright © 2006 Lion Hudson
Text and illustrations copyright: see acknowledgments below

A Lion Children's Book
an imprint of
Lion Hudson plc
Mayfield House, 256 Banbury Road,
Oxford OX2 7DH, England
www.lionhudson.com
ISBN-13 978 0 7459 4648 1
ISBN-10 0 7459 4648 8

First edition 2004
This edition 2006
10 9 8 7 6 5 4 3 2 1 0

Typeset in Baskerville MT Schoolbook
Printed and bound in China

Acknowledgments
Cover (clockwise from top left): Helen Cann, Sarah Young, Carolyn Cox, Clive Scruton, Alex Ayliffe, Christina Balit, Ray and Corrine Burrows, Debbie Lush, John Wallace, Sarah Young. Angel in centre by Sarah Young. Copyright © individual illustrators listed above.
Endpages: 'Christmas Stars' by Lois Rock first published in *A Child's First Book of Prayers*. Text copyright © 2002 Lion Hudson. Illustrations for 'Christmas Stars' from *A First Look: Prayer* and for 'Come Again' from *Ready, Steady Christmas!* copyright © 1996 and 1999 Carolyn Cox.
Christmas Is Coming: Text by Lois Rock first published in *The Lion Book of 1000 Prayers for Children*. Copyright © 2003 Lion Hudson. Illustrations from *This Amazing World* copyright © 2002 Ruth Rivers.
The Story of the Nativity: First published in *Best-Loved Carols*. Copyright © 1998 Lion Hudson. Illustrations copyright © 1998 Debbie Lush.
Mary Had a Baby: First published in *Best-Loved Carols*. Copyright © 1998 Lion Hudson. Arranged by Philip and Victoria Tebbs. Illustrations copyright © 1998 Debbie Lush.
Baby Jesus: Text by Lois Rock first published in *My Very First Bible*. Copyright © 2003 Lion Hudson. Illustrations copyright © 2003 Alex Ayliffe.
Little Angels: Text by Christina Goodings first published in *Baby Rhymes and Bedtime Blessings*. Copyright © 1999 Lion Hudson. Illustrations copyright © 1999 Alex Ayliffe.
Teddy Bear, Piglet, Kitten and Me: First published by Lion as a picture story book with this title in 2000. Text copyright © 2000 Catherine Maccabe. Illustrations copyright © 2000 Clive Scruton.

Let Us Travel to Christmas: Poem with this title by Lois Rock first published in *The Lion Book of 1000 Prayers for Children*. Copyright © 2003 Lion Hudson. The other three poems were first published in *Christmas Rhymes and Carols*, compiled by Lois Rock. Copyright © 2000 Lion Hudson. Illustrations copyright © 2000 John Wallace.
The Fourth Wise Man: Text by Lois Rock first published in *The Lion Book of Tales and Legends*. Copyright © 2003 Lion Hudson. Illustrations copyright © 2003 Christina Balit.
The Gifts of Christmas: Text by Lois Rock first published in *What Will You Wear to Go Swimming?* Copyright © 2002 Lion Hudson. Illustrations from *Words of Gold* copyright © 1997 Sarah Young.
Baboushka: First published by Lion as a picture story book with this title in 1982. Text copyright © 1982, 1989, 2001 Arthur Scholey. Illustrations copyright © 1982 Ray and Corrine Burrows.
The Legend of Saint Nicholas: Text by Lois Rock first published in *Celebrating Christmas*. Copyright © 1998 Lion Hudson. Illustrations copyright © 1998 Helen Cann.
Brother Comgall's Christmas: First published in *The Lion Storyteller Christmas Book*. Text copyright © 2000 Bob Hartman. Illustrations copyright © 2000 Susie Poole.
Papa Panov's Special Day: First published by Lion as a picture story book with this title in 1976. Text copyright © 1976 Mig Holder. Illustrations copyright © 1988 Tony Morris.
Heaven on Earth: 'May the world turn round about' by Lois Rock first published in *The Lion Book of 1000 Prayers for Children*. Copyright © 2003 Lion Hudson. Illustrations from *Heaven in a Poem* copyright © 2000 Christopher Corr.

Come Again

Noël is leaving us,
Sad 'tis to tell,
But he will come again,
Goodbye, Noël.
The kings ride away
In the snow and the rain,
After twelve months
We shall see them again.

Traditional French

All Lion books are available from your local bookshop, or can be ordered via our website or from Marston Book Services. For a free catalogue, showing the complete list of titles available, please contact:

Customer Services
Marston Book Services
PO Box 269
Abingdon
Oxon
OX14 4YN

Tel: 01235 465500
Fax: 01235 465555

Our website can be found at:
www.lionhudson.com